W9-CHX-107

MAYA EMPIRE

Virginia Loh-Hagan

45TH PARALLEL PRESS

Published in the United States of America by Cherry Lake Publishing Group
Ann Arbor, Michigan
www.cherrylakepublishing.com
Reading Adviser: Marla Conn, MS, Ed., Literacy specialist, Read-Ability, Inc.

Book Designer: Melinda Millward

Photo Credits: © gary718/Shutterstock.com, cover, 1; © Lanmas / Alamy Stock Photo, 4; © shadiego/
Shutterstock.com, 6; © Kertu/Shutterstock.com, 8; © Natalya Erofeeva/Shutterstock.com, 10; © Leonid
Andronov/Shutterstock.com, 12; © soft_light/Shutterstock.com, 14; © AntonBkrd/Shutterstock.com,
16; © pop_gino /Adobe Stock, back cover, 18; © NNNMMM/Shutterstock.com, 20; © Vlad Ghiea /
Dreamstime.com, 22; © Photo Beto/istockphoto.com, 24; © NadyaRa/Shutterstock.com, 27; © Matyas
Rehak/Shutterstock.com, 28

Graphic Element Credits: © Milos Djapovic/Shutterstock.com, back cover, front cover; © cajoer/
Shutterstock.com, back cover, front cover, multiple interior pages; © GUSAK OLENA/Shutterstock.com,
back cover, multiple interior pages; © Miloje/Shutterstock.com, front cover; © Rtstudio/Shutterstock.
com, multiple interior pages; © Konstantin Nikiteev/Dreamstime.com, 29

Library of Congress Cataloging-in-Publication Data

Names: Loh-Hagan, Virginia, author.
Title: Maya Empire / by Virginia Loh-Hagan.
Description: Ann Arbor, Michigan : Cherry Lake Publishing, [2021] | Series: Surviving history | Includes
   index.
Identifiers: LCCN 2020003304 (print) | LCCN 2020003305 (ebook) | ISBN 9781534169104 (hardcover)
   | ISBN 9781534170780 (paperback) | ISBN 9781534172623 (pdf) | ISBN 9781534174467 (ebook)
Subjects: LCSH: Mayas—Juvenile literature.
Classification: LCC F1435 .L82 2021 (print) | LCC F1435 (ebook) | DDC 972.81—dc23
LC record available at https://lccn.loc.gov/2020003304
LC ebook record available at https://lccn.loc.gov/2020003305

Printed in the United States of America
Corporate Graphics

TABLE OF CONTENTS

INTRODUCTION

Ancient Mayan kings ruled the empire. They got their power from Mayan gods.

The **ancient** Maya **Empire** developed in what are now Guatemala, Belize, and southern Mexico. Ancient means from a time long ago. An empire is a group of nations ruled by one leader. The Maya Empire was most powerful around the 6th century. Most Mayan cities were **abandoned** in the 10th century. Abandoned means left behind.

Ancient Mayans lived in the Yucatan **Peninsula**. A peninsula is like an island connected to land. This meant ancient Mayans were centered in one area. They were safe from invasions. But they did battle with other **tribes**. Tribes are groups of people. Ancient Mayans fought to protect their lands. They fought to gain more lands.

Mayan pyramids were copies of the Mayan gods' mountains.

Ancient Mayans were great builders. They built **pyramids**. Pyramids are large buildings. They have square bases. They have sloping sides. The sides meet at a point. Ancient Mayans also built **monuments**. Monuments are large structures. They honor someone. Ancient Mayans built temples. They built palaces. Their cities were called stone cities. Around the cities were farms. Ancient Mayans were great farmers as well.

Ancient Mayans worshipped many gods. They created a system of law and order. They created a writing system. They made paper from tree bark. They wrote books. They studied stars and invented a calendar. They invented a number system. They invented chocolate. They invented rubber. They created art. They were great weavers. They were great potters.

NOBLE OR NOT?

Ancient Mayans used body paint.

Ancient Mayans had specific ideas about beauty. They changed the shape of their babies' heads. Head shapes were signs of social class. Children belonged to the class of their parents. Mayan parents made a special headband. They bound 2 boards to their babies' heads. They added pressure over time. This flattened babies' skulls. Ancient Mayans did this to worship Yum Kaax. Yum Kaax was the corn god. Corn narrows at the top. This is why long heads were signs of beauty.

Ancient Mayans pierced their ears, lips, and noses. They wore jewelry. They also drilled holes in their front teeth. They put gems in the holes. They also filed teeth to make them pointy. They thought crossed eyes were beautiful. They thought big noses were beautiful.

QUESTION 1

What type of head shape would you have had?

A You were the child of a **noble**. Nobles are royal people. They're rich. They're the highest class. Their heads were higher and more pointed than priests. They reached the skies. They were shaped to honor the gods. This was so they looked more noble to the gods.

B You were the child of a **priest**. Priests are religious leaders. Their heads were high and pointed.

C You were the child of a worker. Your head was formed into a round shape. Your sides were flattened.

Some people thought ancient Mayans were aliens. This was due to their long heads.

SURVIVOR BIOGRAPHY

Lady Six Sky was an ancient Mayan queen. She ruled from 682 to 741 CE. She ruled Naranjo. Naranjo was an ancient city in Guatemala. It was built on a hill. It had a small cave at the bottom. Lady Six Sky created a new dynasty. Dynasties are ruling families. Lady Six Sky was part of an arranged marriage. She married the Naranjo king to make peace. Her son became the next king. Several monuments honor Lady Six Sky. They show her performing important rites. They show her standing over prisoners of war. This means she took over the role of a warrior-king. This was unusual for women at the time. Lady Six Sky's rule was longer than other Mayan queens. She had a lot of power. She won at least 8 military attacks. She kept her city united.

WIN OR LOSE?

Tikal National Park is in Guatemala. It has 5 ancient ball courts.

Ancient Mayans played a ball game. They passed a heavy rubber ball. They passed the ball without using their hands. Their goal was to get the ball through a stone hoop. Ancient Mayans wore gear to protect themselves. They protected their ribs. They protected their knees. They protected their arms.

This was a tough game. It was deadly. Ancient Mayans played for their lives. Winners could live. Losers were killed.

The ball game was inspired by a Mayan **myth**. Myths are stories. In the story, 2 brothers fought **underworld** lords. The underworld is the place where souls of dead people live. The brothers and lords played a ball game. The brothers won.

QUESTION 2

What type of ballplayer would you have been?

A You were a woman. Only men played this game.

B You were a **professional** player. Professionals have experience and training. You were a Mayan warrior. You wore jade necklaces. You wore scary face paint. You were skilled at aiming the ball using your elbows, legs, and shoulders.

C You had little experience with the game. You did not know all the rules. You were a prisoner of war. This means you were forced to play.

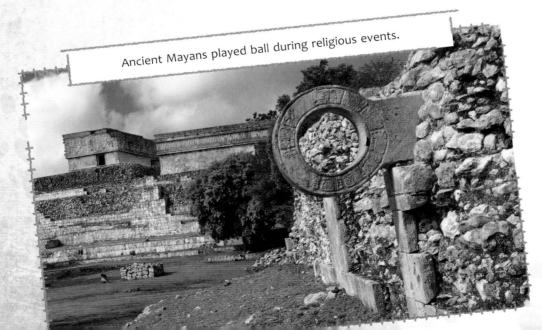

Ancient Mayans played ball during religious events.

SURVIVAL BY THE NUMBERS

- Today, about 30 Mayan languages have survived. They're spoken by over 5 million people. Most of these people can also speak Spanish.
- Ancient Mayan civilization consisted of over 40 cities. Each city had about 5,000 to 50,000 people.
- By 950 CE, 90 to 95 percent of ancient Mayans had died.
- About 40 percent of people in Guatemala today can trace their family roots to the ancient Mayans.
- Ancient Mayans believed there were 9 levels of the underworld. The underworld was ruled by 9 to 14 gods. After the nineth level, there were 13 more levels of higher afterlife.
- El Mirador was one of ancient Maya's greatest cities. Today, it's a lost city. Jungle now covers the city. El Mirador was home to 200,000 people. It's home to 3 pyramids. The largest pyramid is La Danta. It's 230 feet (70 meters) tall. It took 15 million days of work to build.

LIVE OR DIE?

Maya blue is a color of **pigment**. Pigments can be used as paint. It was found on stone monuments. It survived thousands of years.

Maya blue is a lively blue color. It was used in ancient Mayan human **sacrifice**. Sacrifices are acts of killing humans. Humans were given as offerings to gods. Ancient Mayans made sacrifices to please rain gods. They painted human sacrifices blue.

Ancient Mayans killed their sacrifices in different ways. They cut out hearts. They cut off heads. They threw their sacrifices down wells. They sacrificed them in special events. They did this in front of everyone.

Ancient Mayans used different people as sacrifices. They used the losers of ball games. They used prisoners of war. They ate the hearts of enemy warriors. This was to gain their power.

QUESTION 3

Would you have been a human sacrifice?

A You were an enemy soldier. You lost the battle. Enemy soldiers were forced to be **slaves**. Slaves are people forced to work for free.

B You were a noble or king from a neighboring village. You were taken as a **captive**. Captive means to be a prisoner. Captives were forced to play a ball game. If they won, they could live. They'd become slaves. If they lost, they'd be killed.

C You were a young boy. Young boys were offered to the rain gods. It was a great honor to be sacrificed.

Ball games represented battles. A priest would cut out the heart of the loser.

SURVIVAL TIPS

Follow these tips to survive extreme sports:

- Do warm-up exercises. Get your body ready for extreme sports. Stretching warms up muscles.
- Don't overdo it. Be gentle to your body. Don't play if you're in pain.
- Cool down after extreme sports. Walk or jog. Do stretches.
- Learn how to fall. Bend your knees. Avoid twisting arms or legs. Protect bones and muscles. Try to fall on your side or bottom. Roll over naturally. Turn your head in the direction of the roll.
- Wear the right shoes. Wear protective gear. Use helmets. Use goggles. Use padding.
- Take lots of water breaks. Avoid being dehydrated. Avoid overheating.
- See a doctor before doing extreme sports.
- Know the rules of the game. Listen to your coach.
- Don't do extreme sports alone. Have a buddy. Let them know what you're doing.

WET OR DRY?

Chaac was a Mayan rain god. He used a lightning axe to strike the clouds. That's how he made thunder and rain.

Droughts are periods of low rainfall. Without rain, there'd be no water. Without water, there'd be no crops. Without crops, there'd be no food. Without food, people would die.

Ancient Mayans lived in a rainforest. But their land was more like a desert. They relied on rain for water. There were several droughts. This made life hard for ancient Mayans.

The ancient Maya Empire grew. There were more people. More people needed more resources. There were only so many resources left. Droughts reduced the resources. Ancient Mayans had to move or die. Droughts helped cause the end of the Maya Empire.

QUESTION 4

Would you have survived the droughts?

A You carefully checked trees' growth cycles. You kept track of the rainfall. You left the Maya Empire when droughts hit. You joined other tribes that lived by water.

B You were an ancient Mayan builder. You burned and chopped down trees. You did this to clear lands for farming. Without trees, water **evaporates** less. Evaporate means when water turns into gas. This reduces clouds and rainfall.

C You didn't want to leave your home. You stayed in the Maya Empire. You had a hard time finding food.

Many ancient Mayans left the empire.
They became part of other tribes.

SURVIVAL TOOLS

The Yucatan Peninsula has limited water sources. People need water to survive. Ancient Mayans relied on cenotes. Cenotes were underground caves. They held water. Ancient Mayans made the caves bigger. This was so they could get to the water. Ancient Mayans created villages near cenotes. They kept these sacred water holes secret. They also used natural dips in the ground. These dips held rainwater. Ancient Mayans became excellent managers of rainwater. In areas without cenotes, they developed chultans. Chultans were tanks for storing water. They were shaped like bottles. They were underground. They were lined with plaster. Rains fell. They were guided into the chultans.

TO PARADISE OR BUST?

Ancient Mayans worshipped their ancestors. Ancestors are family members who came before us.

Ancient Mayans respected death. They thought certain deaths were more noble than others. They had many rites to honor deaths. They put corn in the mouths of dead bodies. The corn-fed dead souls traveled to the underworld.

This underworld was called Xibalba. It had a tree of life. This tree came through the earth. It spread to the top of mountains. At the top was **paradise**. Paradise is a perfect place. In paradise, everyone is happy.

After dying, ancient Mayans went on a journey. They had to fight demons. They fought to keep their souls. They traveled to paradise.

QUESTION 5

Would you have had a noble ancient Mayan death?

A You died as a sacrifice. You died giving birth. You died in battle. If so, you were sent directly to paradise. Ancient Mayans honored violent deaths. Their gods were grateful for your effort.

B You were a member of the royal family. You were wrapped in cloth. The cloth kept you in a tight space. It ensured safe travel to the underworld.

C You were a captive. You were a **foreigner**. Foreigners are people from different places. They were buried naked. Mayans believed this made it harder for the soul to find paradise.

Ancient Mayans believed that souls
were bound to bodies at birth.

SURVIVAL RESULTS

Murder was not common in the ancient Maya Empire.
The punishment for murder was extreme.

Would you have survived?

Find out! Add up your answers to the chapter questions. Did you have more **A**s, **B**s, or **C**s?

- If you had more **A**s, then you're a survivor! Congrats!

- If you had more **B**s, then you're on the edge. With some luck, you might have just made it.

- If you had more **C**s, then you wouldn't have survived.

Are you happy with your results? Did you have a tie? Sometimes fate is already decided for us. Follow the link below to our webpage. Scroll until you find the series name *Surviving History*. Click download. Print out the template. Follow the directions to create your own paper die. Read the book again. Roll the die to find your new answers. Did your fate change?

https://cherrylakepublishing.com/teaching_guides

DIGGING DEEPER: DID YOU KNOW…?

The ancient Maya Empire was exciting. Ancient Mayans achieved great things. But many lives were lost as well. Surviving history involves many different factors. Dig deeper. Consider some of the facts below.

QUESTION 1:

What type of head shape would you have had?

- Babies' heads are soft. This is why they can be shaped.
- Some people think ancient Mayan heads were shaped to look like a jaguar's head.
- Experts study ancient Mayan skulls.

QUESTION 2:

What type of ballplayer would you have been?

- Teams had 2 or 3 players.
- Some ancient Mayans bet on the games.
- The ball could break bones.

QUESTION 3:

Would you have been a human sacrifice?

- Human sacrifices were done to celebrate new rulers.
- Human sacrifices were done to celebrate a new temple.
- People who were sacrificed wore headdresses. They were held down by 4 people.

QUESTION 4:

Would you have survived the droughts?

- The Yucatan had dry and wet seasons. Droughts brought more dry seasons.
- Some droughts lasted 2 to 20 years.
- Ancient Mayan traders were affected by the droughts. Their trading routes dried up. Without crops, they didn't have much to trade.

QUESTION 5:

Would you have had a noble ancient Mayan death?

- Ancient Mayans built statues of their dead family members.
- Graves faced north or west. This was in the directions of the Mayan heavens. Other graves were in caves. Caves were thought to be doors to the underworld.
- Some people sacrificed dogs. Dogs were thought to help dead souls travel to paradise.

GLOSSARY

abandoned (uh-BAN-duhnd) left behind
ancient (AYN-shuhnt) from a time long ago
captive (KAP-tiv) prisoner
droughts (DROUTS) periods of low rainfall
empire (EM-pire) group of nations ruled by one leader
evaporates (ih-VAP-uh-rates) turns from liquid into gas
foreigner (FOR-uh-nur) person from a faraway place
monuments (MAYN-yuh-muhnts) large buildings that honor someone or something
myth (MITH) cultural story that explained something
noble (NOH-buhl) rich, royal person
paradise (PAR-uh-dise) a perfect place
peninsula (puh-NIN-suh-luh) an island connected to land

pigment (PIG-muhnt) a material, used for paint
priest (PREEST) a religious leader
professional (pruh-FESH-uh-nuhl) person who has experience and training
pyramids (PIR-uh-midz) structures with a square base and sloping sides that meet in a point at the top
sacrifice (SAK-ruh-fise) act of killing humans or animals as offerings to the gods
slaves (SLAYVZ) people who are forced to work for free
tribes (TRYBZ) groups of people
underworld (UHN-dur-wurld) place where the souls of dead people live

LEARN MORE!

- Honders, Christine. *Ancient Maya Culture*. New York, NY: PowerKids Press, 2017.
- Somervill, Barbara A. *Ancient Maya*. New York, NY: Children's Press, 2013.
- Williams, Brian. *Maya, Incas, and Aztecs*. New York, NY: DK Publishing, 2018.

INDEX

ABOUT THE AUTHOR

Dr. Virginia Loh-Hagan is an author, university professor, and former classroom teacher. She has traveled to Belize. She visited Mayan temple ruins. She lives in San Diego with her very tall husband and very naughty dogs. To learn more about her, visit www.virginialoh.com.